FALLACIES OF
ANTI-REFORMERS

BY

SYDNEY SMITH

British Library Cataloguing-in-Publication Data
A catalogue record for this book is available from the
British Library

Sydney Smith

Sydney Smith was born on 3rd June 1771 in Woodford, Essex, England.

Smith was educated at Winchester College, where he greatly distinguished himself, rising to the position of school captain. In fact, he and his brother were so recognised for thier all-round abilities that their school fellows signed a round-robin "refusing to try for the college prizes if the Smiths were allowed to contend for them anymore".

In 1789, upon leaving Winchester College, he became a scholar at New College, Oxford. He received a fellowship from the college and finally obtained his Master of Arts degree in 1796. Smith's intention was to go on to read for the bar, but his father refused and compelled him to join the clergy. He was ordained at Oxford in 1796 and became the curate of the village of Netheravon, near Amesbury in Salisbury Plain. The squire of the parish engaged Smith to tutor his son and the pair went to Edinburgh to study. While his pupil attended lectures, Smith studied moral philosophy, medicine, and chemistry.

Smith's first book 'Six Sermons, preached in Charlotte Street Chapel, Edinburgh' was published in 1800. He married Catharine Amelia Pybus in the same year and the couple settled in Edinburgh. While there, he helped set up the *Edinburgh Review* and became its first editor in 1802. He continued to write articles for the review for the next quarter of the century which were a key element to the publication's success.

Smith left Scotland in 1803 and relocated to London. He became well known as a preacher, lecturer, and society figure, and he often preached to huge crowds in Berkeley Chapel, Mayfair.. He lectured at the Royal Institution on moral philosophy and promoted progressive values such as the education of women and the abolition of slavery. He often destroyed paper copies of his lectures after they had served their purpose but his wife rescued some of the charred manuscripts and published them as 'Elementary Sketches of Moral Philosophy' in 1850.

His most famous work is *Peter Plymley's Letters* (1892) in which he deals with the subject of Catholic emancipation, ridiculing the opposition of the country clergy.

Smith continued his career in the church, preaching in Yorkshire for twenty years and being appointed to a residentiary canonry at St Paul's Cathedral in 1831.

He is remembered as a fine wit and humourist, and is often quoted in English literary life. Smith died on 22nd February 1845.

There[1] are a vast number of absurd and mischievous fallacies, which pass readily in the world for sense and virtue, while in truth they tend only to fortify error and encourage crime. Mr. Bentham has enumerated the most conspicuous of these in the book before us.

Whether it be necessary there should be a middleman between the cultivator and the possessor, learned economists have doubted; but neither gods, men, nor booksellers can doubt the necessity of a middleman between Mr. Bentham and the public. Mr. Bentham is long; Mr. Bentham is occasionally involved and obscure; Mr. Bentham invents new and alarming expressions; Mr. Bentham loves division and subdivision—and he loves method itself, more than its consequences. Those only, therefore, who know his originality, his knowledge, his vigor, and his boldness, will recur to the works themselves. The great mass of readers will not purchase improvement at so dear a rate; but will choose rather to become acquainted with Mr. Bentham through the medium of reviews—after that eminent philosopher has been washed, trimmed, shaved, and forced into clean linen. One great use of a review, indeed, is to make men wise in ten pages, who have no appetite for a hundred pages; to condense nourishment, to work with pulp and essence, and to guard the stomach from idle burden and unmeaning bulk. For half a page, sometimes for a whole page, Mr. Bentham writes with a power which few can equal; and by selecting and omitting, an admirable style may be formed from the text. Using this liberty, we shall endeavor to give an account of Mr. Bentham's doctrines, for the most part in his own words. Wherever an expression is particularly happy, let it be considered to be Mr. Bentham's—the dullness we take to ourselves.

OUR WISE ANCESTORS—*The Wisdom of Our Ancestors—The Wisdom of Ages Venerable Antiquity—Wisdom of Old Times.*—This mischievous and absurd fallacy springs from the grossest perversion of the meaning of words. Experience is certainly the mother of wisdom, and the old have, of course, a greater experience than the young; but the question is who are the old? and who are the young? Of *individuals* living at the same period, the oldest has, of course, the greatest experience; but among *generations* of men the reverse of this is true. Those who come first (our ancestors) are the young people, and have the least experience. We have added to their experience the experience of many centuries; and, therefore, as far as experience goes, are wiser, and more capable of forming an opinion than they were. The real feeling should be, *not* can we be so presumptuous as to put our opinions in opposition to those of our ancestors?

but can such young, ignorant, inexperienced persons as our ancestors necessarily were, be expected to have understood a subject as well as those who have seen so much more, lived so much longer, and enjoyed the experience of so many centuries? All this cant, then, about our ancestors is merely an abuse of words, by transferring phrases true of contemporary men to succeeding ages. Whereas (as we have before observed) of living men the oldest has, *cæteris paribus*,[2] the most experience; of generations, the oldest has *cæteris paribus*, the least experience. Our ancestors, up to the Conquest, were children in arms; chubby boys in the time of Edward I; striplings under Elizabeth; men in the reign of Queen Anne; and *we* only are the white-bearded, silver-headed ancients, who have treasured up, and are prepared to profit by, all the experience which human life can supply. We are not disputing with our ancestors the palm of talent, in which they may or may not be our superiors, but the palm of experience in which it is utterly impossible they can be our superiors. And yet, whenever the Chancellor comes forward to protect some abuse, or to oppose some plan which has the increase of human happiness for its object, his first appeal is always to the wisdom of our ancestors; and he himself, and many noble lords who vote with him, are, to this hour, persuaded that all alterations and amendments on their devices are an unblushing controversy between youthful temerity and mature experience!—and so, in truth they are—only that much-loved magistrate mistakes the young for the old, and the old for the young—and is guilty of that very sin against experience which he attributes to the lovers of innovation.

We cannot of course be supposed to maintain that our ancestors wanted wisdom, or that they were necessarily mistaken in their institutions, because their means of information were more limited than ours. But we do confidently maintain that when we find it expedient to change anything which our ancestors have enacted, we are the experienced persons, and not they. The quantity of talent is always varying in any great nation. To say that we are more or less able than our ancestors is an assertion that requires to be explained. All the able men of all ages, who have ever lived in England, probably possessed, if taken altogether, more intellect than all the able men England can now boast of. But if authority must be resorted to rather than reason, the question is, What was the wisdom of the single age which enacted the law, compared with the wisdom of the age which proposes to alter it? What are the eminent men of one and the other period? If you say that our ancestors were wiser than us, mention your date and year. If the splendor of names is equal, are the circumstances the same? If the circumstances are the same, we have a superiority of experience, of which the difference between the two periods is the measure. It is necessary to insist upon this; for upon sacks of wool, and on benches forensic, sit grave men, and agricolous persons in the Commons, crying out: "Ancestors, ancestors! *hodie non!*[β] Saxons, Danes, save us! Fiddlefrig, help us! Howel, Ethelwolf, protect us!" Any cover for nonsense—any veil for trash—any pretext for repelling the innovations of conscience and of duty!

"So long as they keep to vague generalities—so long as the two objects of comparison are each of them taken in the lump—wise ancestors in one lump, ignorant and foolish mob of modern times in the other—the weakness of the fallacy may escape detection. But let them assign for the period of superior wisdom any determinate period whatsoever, not only will the groundlessness of the notion be apparent (class being compared with class in that period and the present one), but unless the antecedent period be comparatively speaking a very modern one, so wide will be the disparity, and to such an amount in favor of modern times, that, in comparison of the lowest class of the people in modern times (always supposing them proficient in the art of reading, and their proficiency employed in the reading of newspapers), the very highest and best-informed class of these wise ancestors will turn out to be grossly ignorant.

"Take, for example, any year in the reign of Henry VIII, from 1509 to 1546. At that time the House of Lords would probably have been in possession of by far the larger proportion of what little instruction the age afforded; in the

House of Lords, among the laity, it might even then be a question whether, without exception, their lordships were all of them able so much as to read. But even supposing them all in the fullest possession of that useful art, political science being the science in question, what instruction on the subject could they meet with at that time of day?

"On no one branch of legislation was any book extant from which, with regard to the circumstances of the then present times, any useful instruction could be derived: distributive law, penal law, international law, political economy, so far from existing as sciences, had scarcely obtained a name: in all those departments under the head of *quid faciendum*, a mere blank: the whole literature of the age consisted of a meagre chronicle or two, containing short memorandums of the usual occurrences of war and peace, battles, sieges, executions, revels, deaths, births, processions, ceremonies, and other external events; but with scarce a speech or an incident that could enter into the composition of any such work as a history of the human mind—with scarce an attempt at investigation into causes, characters, or the state of the people at large. Even when at last, little by little, a scrap or two of political instruction came to be obtainable, the proportion of error and mischievous doctrine mixed up with it was so great, that whether a blank unfilled might not have been less prejudicial than a blank thus filled, may reasonably be matter of doubt.

"If we come down to the reign of James I, we shall find that Solomon of his time eminently eloquent as well as learned, not only among crowned but among uncrowned heads, marking out for prohibition and punishment the practices of devils and witches, and without the slightest objection on the part of the great characters of that day in their high situations, consigning men to death and torment for the misfortune of not being so well acquainted as he was with the composition of the Godhead.

"Under the name of exorcism the Catholic liturgy contains a form of procedure for driving out devils;—even with the help of this instrument, the operation cannot be performed with the desired success, but by an operator qualified by holy orders for the working of this as well as so many other wonders. In our days and in our country the same object is attained, and beyond comparison more effectually, by so cheap an instrument as a common newspaper; before this talisman, not only devils but ghosts, vampires, witches, and all their kindred tribes, are driven out of the land, never to return again! The touch of holy water is not so intolerable to them as the bare smell of printers' ink."[4]

FALLACY OF IRREVOCABLE LAWS.—A law, says Mr. Bentham (no matter to what effect) is proposed to a legislative assembly, who are called upon to reject it, upon the single ground that by those who in some former period exercised the same power, a regulation was made, having for its object to preclude forever, or to the end of an unexpired period, all succeeding legislators from enacting a law to any such effect as that now proposed.

Now it appears quite evident that, at every period of time, every legislature must be endowed with all those powers which the exigency of the times may require; and any attempt to infringe on this power is inadmissible and absurd. The sovereign power, at any one period, can only form a blind guess at the measures which may be necessary for any future period; but by this principle of immutable laws, the government is transferred from those who are necessarily the best judges of what they want, to others who can know little or nothing about the matter. The thirteenth century decides for the fourteenth. The fourteenth makes laws for the fifteenth. The fifteenth hermetically seals up the sixteenth, which tyrannizes over the seventeenth, which again tells the eighteenth how it is to act, under circumstances which cannot be foreseen, and how it is to conduct itself in exigencies which no human wit can anticipate.

"Men who have a century more experience to ground their judgments on, surrender their intellect to men who had a century less experience, and who, unless that deficiency constitutes a claim, have no claim to preference. If the prior generation were, in respect of intellectual qualification, ever so much superior to the subsequent generation—if it understood so much better than the subsequent generation itself the interest of that subsequent generation—could it have been in an equal degree anxious to promote that interest, and consequently equally attentive to those facts with which, though in order to form a judgment it ought to have been, it is impossible that it should have been, acquainted? In a word, will its love for that subsequent generation be quite so great as that same generation's love for itself?

"Not even here, after a moment's deliberate reflection, will the assertion be in the affirmative. And yet it is their prodigious anxiety for the welfare of their posterity that produces the propensity of these sages to tie up the hands of this same posterity forever more—to act as guardians to its perpetual and incurable weakness, and take its conduct forever out of its own hands.

"If it be right that the conduct of the nineteenth century should be determined not by its own judgment but by that of the eighteenth, it will be equally right that the conduct of the twentieth century should be determined not by its own judgment but by that of the nineteenth. And if the same principle were still pursued, what at length would be the consequence?—that in process of time the practice of legislation would be at an end. The conduct and fate of all men would be determined by those who neither knew nor cared anything about the matter; and the aggregate body of the living would remain forever in subjection to

11

an inexorable tyranny, exercised as it were by the aggregate body of the Dead."[5]

The despotism, as Mr. Bentham well observes, of Nero or Caligula would be more tolerable than an "irrevocable law." The despot, through fear or favor, or in a lucid interval, might relent; but how are the Parliament who made the Scotch Union, for example, to be awakened from that dust in which they repose—the jobber and the patriot, the speaker and the doorkeeper, the silent voters and the men of rich allusions, Cannings and cultivators, Barings and beggars—making irrevocable laws for men who toss their remains about with spades, and use the relics of these legislators to give breadth to broccoli, and to aid the vernal eruption of asparagus?

If the law be good, it will support itself; if bad, it should not be supported by "irrevocable theory," which is never resorted to but as the veil of abuses. All living men must possess the supreme power over their own happiness at every particular period. To suppose that there is anything which a whole nation cannot do, which they deem to be essential to their happiness, and that they cannot do it, because *another* generation, long ago dead and gone, said it must not be done, is mere nonsense. While you are captain of the vessel, do what you please; but the moment you quit the ship I become as omnipotent as you. You may leave me as much *advice* as you please, but you cannot leave me *commands*; though, in fact, this is the only meaning which can be applied to what are called irrevocable laws. It appeared to the legislature for the time being to be of immense importance to make such and such a law. Great good was gained, or great evil avoided, by enacting it. Pause before you alter an institution which has been deemed to be of so much importance. This is prudence and common-sense; the rest is the exaggeration of fools, or the artifice of knaves, who eat up fools. What endless nonsense has been talked of our navigation laws! What wealth has been sacrificed to either before they were repealed! How impossible it appeared to Noodledom to repeal them! They were considered of the irrevocable class—a kind of law over which the dead only were omnipotent, and the living had no power. Frost, it is true, cannot be put off by act of Parliament, nor can spring be accelerated by any majority of both houses. It is, however, quite a mistake to suppose that any alteration of any of the articles of union is as much out of the jurisdiction of Parliament as these meteorological changes. In every year, and every day of that year, living men have a right to make their own laws and manage their own affairs; to break through the tyranny of the antespirants— the people who breathed before them—and to do what they please for themselves. Such supreme power cannot indeed be well exercised by the people at large; it must be exercised therefore by the delegates, or Parliament, whom the people choose; and such Parliament, disregarding the superstitious reverence for "irrevocable laws," can have no other criterion of wrong and right than that of public utility.

When a law is considered as immutable, and the immutable law happens at the same time to be too foolish and mischievous to be endured, instead of being repealed, it is clandestinely evaded, or openly violated; and thus the authority of all law is weakened.

Where a nation has been ancestorially bound by foolish and improvident treaties, ample notice must be given of their termination. Where the State has made ill-advised grants, or rash bargains with individuals, it is necessary to grant proper compensation. The most difficult case, certainly, is that of the union of nations, where a smaller number of the weaker nation is admitted into the larger senate of the greater nation, and will be overpowered if the question come to a vote; but the lesser nation must run this risk; it is not probable that any violation of articles will take place till they are absolutely called for by extreme necessity. But let the danger be what it may, no danger is so great, no supposition so foolish, as to consider any human law as irrevocable. The shifting attitude of human affairs would often render such a condition an intolerable evil to all parties. The absurd jealousy of our countrymen at the Union secured heritable jurisdiction to the owners; nine and thirty years afterward they were abolished, in the very teeth of the Act of Union, and to the evident promotion of the public good.

CONTINUITY OF A LAW BY OATH.—The sovereign of England at his coronation takes an oath to maintain the laws of God, the true profession of the Gospel, and the Protestant religion, as established by law, and to preserve to the bishops and clergy of this realm the rights and privileges which by law appertain to them, and to preserve inviolate the doctrine, discipline, worship, and the government of the Church. It has been suggested that by this oath the King stands precluded from granting those indulgences to the Irish Catholics which are included in the bill for their emancipation. The true meaning of these provisions is of course to be decided, if doubtful, by the same legislative authority which enacted them. But a different notion it seems is now afloat. The King for the time being (we are putting an imaginary case) thinks as an individual that he is not maintaining the doctrine, discipline, and rights of the Church of England, if he grant any extension of civil rights to those who are not members of that Church; that he is violating his oath by so doing. This oath, then, according to this reasoning, is the great palladium of the Church. As long as it remains inviolate the Church is safe. How, then, can any monarch who has taken it ever consent to repeal it? How can he, consistently with his oath for the preservation of the privileges of the Church, contribute his part to throw down so strong a bulwark as he deems his oath to be! The oath, then, cannot be altered. It must remain under all circumstances of society the same. The King who has taken it is bound to continue it, and to refuse his sanction to any bill for its future alteration, because it prevents him, and, he must needs think, will prevent others, from granting dangerous immunities to the enemies of the Church.

Here, then, is an irrevocable law—a piece of absurd tyranny exercised by the rulers of Queen Anne's time upon the government of 1825—a certain art of potting and preserving a kingdom in one shape, attitude, and flavor— and in this way it is that an institution appears like old ladies' sweetmeats and made wines—Apricot Jam 1822—Currant Wine 1819—Court of Chancery 1427—Penal Laws against Catholics 1676. The difference is, that the ancient woman is a better judge of mouldy commodities than the illiberal part of his majesty's ministers. The potting lady goes sniffing about and admitting light and air to prevent the progress of decay; while to him of the wool-sack all seems doubly dear in proportion as it is antiquated, worthless, and unusable.

It ought not to be in the power of the sovereign to tie up his own hands, much less the hands of his successors. If the sovereign were to oppose his own opinion to that of the two other branches of the legislature, and himself to decide what he considers to be for the benefit of the Protestant Church, and what not a king who has spent his whole life in the frivolous occupation of a court may by perversion of understanding conceive measures most salutary to the Church to be most

16

pernicious, and, persevering obstinately in his own error, may frustrate the wisdom of his parliament, and perpetuate the most inconceivable folly! If Henry VIII had argued in this manner we should have had no Reformation. If George III had always argued in this manner the Catholic code would never have been relaxed. And thus a King, however incapable of forming an opinion upon serious subjects, has nothing to do but pronounce the word "Conscience," and the whole power of the country is at his feet.

Can there be greater absurdity than to say that a man is acting contrary to his conscience who surrenders his opinion upon any subject to those who must understand the subject better than himself? I think my ward has a claim to the estate; but the best lawyers tell me he has none. I think my son capable of undergoing the fatigues of a military life; but the best physicians say he is much too weak. My Parliament say this measure will do the Church no harm; but I think it very pernicious to the Church. Am I acting contrary to my conscience because I apply much higher intellectual powers than my own to the investigation and protection of these high interests?

"According to the form in which it is conceived, any such engagement is in effect either a check or a license:—a license under the appearance of a check, and for that very reason but the more efficiently operative.

"Chains to the man in power? Yes:—but only such as he figures with on the stage; to the spectators as imposing, to himself as light as possible. Modelled by the wearer to suit his own purposes, they serve to rattle but not to restrain.

"Suppose a king of Great Britain and Ireland to have expressed his fixed determination, in the event of any proposed law being tendered to him for his assent, to refuse such assent, and this not on the persuasion that the law would not be 'for the utility of the subjects,' but that by his coronation oath he stands precluded from so doing, the course proper to be taken by Parliament, the course pointed out by principle and precedent, would be a vote of abdication—a vote declaring the king to have abdicated his royal authority, and that, as in case of death or incurable mental derangement, now is the time for the person next in succession to take his place. In the celebrated case in which a vote to this effect was actually passed, the declaration of abdication was, in lawyers' language, a fiction—in plain truth, a falsehood, and that falsehood a mockery; not a particle of his power was it the wish of James to abdicate, to part with, but to increase it to a maximum was the manifest object of all his efforts. But in the case here supposed, with respect to a part, and that a principal part of the royal authority, the will and purpose to abdicate is actually declared; and this being such a part, without which the remainder cannot, 'to the utility of the subjects,' be exercised, the remainder must of necessity be, on their part and for their sake, added."[6]

SELF-TRUMPETER'S FALLACY.—Mr. Bentham explains the self-trumpeter's fallacy as follows:

"There are certain men in office who, in discharge of their functions, arrogate to themselves a degree of probity, which is to exclude all imputations and all inquiry. Their assertions are to be deemed equivalent to proof, their virtues are guaranties for the faithful discharge of their duties, and the most implicit confidence is to be reposed in them on all occasions. If you expose any abuse, propose any reform, call for securities, inquiry, or measures to promote publicity, they set up a cry of surprise, amounting almost to indignation, as if their integrity were questioned or their honor wounded. With all this, they dexterously mix up intimations that the most exalted patriotism, honor, and perhaps religion, are the only sources of all their actions."[7]

Of course every man will try what he can effect by these means; but (as Mr. Bentham observes) if there be any one maxim in politics more certain than another, it is that no possible degree of virtue in the governor can render it expedient for the governed to dispense with good laws and good institutions. Madame De Staël (to her disgrace) said to the Emperor of Russia: "Sire, your character is a constitution for your country, and your conscience its guaranty." His reply was: "*Quand cela serait, je ne serais jamais qu'un accident*

heureux;"[8] and this we think one of the truest and most
brilliant replies ever made by monarch.

LAUDATORY PERSONALITIES.—"The object of
laudatory personalities is to effect the rejection of a measure
on account of the alleged good character of those who
oppose it, and the argument advanced is: 'The measure is
rendered unnecessary by the virtues of those who are in
power—their opposition is a sufficient authority for the
rejection of the measure. The measure proposed implies a
distrust of the members of his Majesty's Government; but so
great is their integrity, so complete their disinterestedness,
so uniformly do they prefer the public advantage to their
own, that such a measure is altogether unnecessary. Their
disapproval is sufficient to warrant an opposition; precautions
can only be requisite where danger is apprehended; here the
high character of the individuals in question is a sufficient
guaranty against any ground of alarm.'"[9]

The panegyric goes on increasing with the dignity of
the lauded person. All are honorable and delightful men.
The person who opens the door of the office is a person of
approved fidelity; the junior clerk is a model of assiduity;
all the clerks are models—seven years' models, eight years'
models, nine years' models, and upward. The first clerk is a
paragon, and ministers the very perfection of probity and
intelligence; and as for the highest magistrate of the State,
no adulation is equal to describe the extent of his various

merits! It is too condescending, perhaps, to refute such folly as this. But we would just observe that, if the propriety of the measure in question be established by direct arguments, these must be at least as conclusive against the character of those who oppose it as their character can be against the measure.

The effect of such an argument is to give men of good or reputed good character the power of putting a negative on any question not agreeable to their inclinations.

"In every public trust the legislator should for the purpose of prevention, suppose the trustee disposed to break the trust in every imaginable way in which it would be possible for him to reap from the breach of it any personal advantage. This is the principle on which public institutions ought to be formed, and when it is applied to all men indiscriminately, it is injurious to none. The practical inference is to oppose to such possible (and what will always be probable) breaches of trust every bar that can be opposed consistently with the power requisite for the efficient and due discharge of the trust. Indeed, these arguments, drawn from the supposed virtues of men in power, are opposed to the first principles on which all laws proceed.

"Such allegations of individual virtue are never supported by specific proof, are scarce ever susceptible of specific disproof, and specific disproof, if offered, could not be admitted in either House of Parliament. If attempted elsewhere, the punishment would fall not on the unworthy trustee, but on him by whom the unworthiness has been proved."[10]

FALLACIES OF PRETENDED DANGER.— *Imputations of Bad Design; of Bad Character; of Bad Motives; of Inconsistency; of Suspicious Connections.*—The object of this class of fallacies is to draw aside attention from the measure to the man, and this in such a manner that, for some real or supposed defect in the author of the measure, a corresponding defect shall be imputed to the measure itself. Thus, "the author of the measure entertains a bad design; therefore the measure is bad. His character is bad, therefore the measure is bad; his motive is bad, I will vote against the measure. On former occasions this same person who proposed the measure was its enemy, therefore the measure is bad. He is on footing of intimacy with this or that dangerous man, or has been seen in his company, or is suspected of entertaining some of his opinions, therefore the measure is bad. He bears a name that at a former period was borne by a set of men now no more, by whom bad principles were entertained, therefore the measure is bad!"

Now, if the measure be really inexpedient, why not at once show it to be so? If the measure be good, is it bad because a bad man is its author? If bad, is it good because a good man has produced it? What are these arguments but to say to the assembly who are to be the judges of any measure, that their imbecility is too great to allow them to judge of the measure by its own merits, and that they must have recourse to distant and feebler probabilities for that purpose?

"In proportion to the degree of efficiency with which a man suffers these instruments of deception to operate upon his mind, he enables bad men to exercise over him a sort of power, the thought of which ought to cover him with shame. Allow this argument the effect of a conclusive one, you put it into the power of any man to draw you at pleasure from the support of every measure which in your own eyes is good, to force you to give your support to any and every measure which in your own eyes is bad. Is it good?—the bad man embraces it, and by the supposition, you reject it. Is it bad?—he vituperates it, and that suffices for driving you into its embrace. You split upon the rocks because he has avoided them; you miss the harbor because he has steered into it! Give yourself up to any such blind antipathy, you are no less in the power of your adversaries than if, by a correspondently irrational sympathy and obsequiousness, you put yourself into the power of your friends."[11]

"Besides, nothing but laborious application and a clear and comprehensive intellect can enable a man on any given subject to employ successfully relevant arguments drawn from the subject itself. To employ personalities, neither labor or intellect is required. In this sort of contest the most idle and the most ignorant are quite on a par with, if not superior to, the most industrious and the most highly gifted individuals. Nothing can be more convenient for those who would speak without the trouble of thinking. The same ideas are brought forward over and over again, and all that is required is to very the turn of expression. Close and relevant arguments have very little hold on the passions, and serve rather to quell than to inflame them; while in personalities there is always something stimulant, whether on the part of him who praises or him who blames. Praise forms a kind of connection between the party praising and the party praised, and vituperation gives an air of courage and independence to the party who blames.

"Ignorance and indolence, friendship and enmity, concurring and conflicting interest, servility and independence, all conspire to give personalities the ascendency they so unhappily maintain. The more we lie under the influence of our own passions, the more we rely on others being affected in a similar degree. A man who can repel these injuries with dignity may often convert them into triumph: 'Strike me, but hear,' says he, and the fury of his antagonist redounds to his own discomfiture."[12]

NO INNOVATION!—To say that all things new are bad is to say that all old things were bad in their commencement: for of all the old things ever seen or heard of there is not one that was not once new. Whatever is now establishment was once innovation. The first inventor of pews and parish clerks was no doubt considered as a Jacobin in his day. Judges, juries, criers of the court, are all the inventions of ardent spirits, who filled the world with alarm, and were considered as the great precursors of ruin and dissolution. No inoculation, no turnpikes, no reading, no writing, no popery! The fool sayeth in his heart and crieth with his mouth, "I will have nothing new!"

FALLACY OF DISTRUST!—*"What's at the Bottom?"*— This fallacy begins with a virtual admission of the propriety of the measure considered in itself, and thus demonstrates its own futility, and cuts up from under itself the ground which it endeavours to make. A measure is to be rejected for something that, by bare possibility, may be found amiss in some other measure! This is vicarious reprobation; upon this principle Herod instituted his massacre. It is the argument of a driveller to other drivellers, who says: "We are not able to decide upon the evil when it arises; our only safe way is to act upon the general apprehension of evil."

OFFICIAL MALEFACTOR'S SCREEN—*"Attack Us, You Attack Government."*—If this notion is acceded to, everyone who derives at present any advantage from misrule has it in fee-simple, and all abuses, present and future, are without remedy. So long as there is anything amiss in conducting the business of government, so long as it can be made better, there can be no other mode of bringing it nearer to perfection than the indication of such imperfections as at the time being exist.

"But so far is it from being true that a man's aversion or contempt for the hands by which the powers of government, or even for the system under which they are exercised, is a proof of his aversion or contempt toward government itself, that, even in proportion to the strength of that aversion or contempt, it is a proof of the opposite affection. What, in consequence of such contempt or aversion, he wishes for is not that there be no hands at all to exercise these powers, but that the hands may be better regulated;—not that those powers should not be exercised at all, but that they should be better exercised;—not that in the exercise of them no rules at all should be pursued, but that the rules by which they are exercised should be a better set of rules.

"All government is a trust, every branch of government is a trust, and immemorially acknowledged so to be; it is only by the magnitude of the scale that public differ from private trusts. I complain of the conduct of a person in the character of guardian, as domestic guardian, having the care of a minor or insane person. In so doing do I say that guardianship is a bad institution? Does it enter into the head of anyone to suspect me of so doing? I complain of an individual in the character of a commercial agent or assignee of the effects of an insolvent. In so doing do I say that commercial agency is a bad thing? that the practice of vesting in the hands of trustees or assignees the effects of an insolvent for the purpose of their being divided among his creditors is a bad practice? Does any such conceit ever enter into the head of man as that of suspecting me of so doing."[13]

There are no complaints against government in Turkey—no motions in Parliament, no "Morning Chronicles," and no "Edinburgh Reviews": yet of all countries in the world it is that in which revolts and revolutions are the most frequent.

It is so far from true that no good government can exist consistently with such disclosure, that no good government can exist without it. It is quite obvious to all who are capable of reflection that by no other means than by lowering the governors in the estimation of the people can there be hope or chance of beneficial change. To infer from this wise endeavor to lessen the existing rulers in the estimation of the people, a wish of dissolving the government, is either artifice or error. The physician who intentionally weakens the patient by bleeding him has no intention he should perish.

The greater the quantity of respect a man receives, independently of good conduct, the less good is his behavior likely to be. It is the interest, therefore, of the public in the case of each to see that the respect paid to him should, as completely as possible, depend upon the goodness of his behavior in the execution of his trust. But it is, on the contrary, the interest of the trustee that the respect, the money, or any other advantage he receives in virtue of his office, should be as great, as secure, and as independent of conduct as possible. Soldiers expect to be shot at; public men must expect to be attacked, and sometimes unjustly. It keeps up the habit of considering their conduct as exposed to scrutiny; on the part of the people at large it keeps alive the expectation of witnessing such attacks, and the habit of looking out for them. The friends and supporters of government have always greater facility in keeping and raising it up than its adversaries have for lowering it.

ACCUSATION-SCARER'S DEVICE—*"Infamy Must Attach Somewhere."*—This fallacy consists in representing the character of a calumniator as necessarily and justly attaching upon him who, having made a charge of misconduct against any person possessed of political power or influence, fails of producing evidence sufficient for their conviction.

"If taken as a general proposition, applying to all public accusations, nothing can be more mischievous as well as fallacious. Supposing the charge unfounded, the delivery of it may have been accompanied with *mala fides* (consciousness of its injustice), with *temerity* only, or it may have been perfectly blameless. It is in the first case alone that infamy can with propriety attach upon him who brings it forward. A charge really groundless may have been honestly *believed* to be well founded, *i. e.*, believed with a sort of provisional credence, sufficient for the purpose of engaging a man to do his part toward the bringing about an investigation, but without sufficient reasons. But a charge may be perfectly groundless without attaching the smallest particle of blame upon him who brings it forward. Suppose him to have heard from one or more, presenting themselves to him in the character of percipient witnesses, a story which, either *in toto*, or perhaps only in *circumstances*, though in circumstances of the most material importance, should prove false and mendacious, how is the person who hears this and acts accordingly to blame? What sagacity can enable a man previously to legal investigation, a man who has no power that can enable him to insure correctness or completeness on the part of this extrajudicial testimony, to guard against deception in such a case?"[14]

FALLACY OF FALSE CONSOLATION—"*What is the Matter with You?—What Would You Have?—Look at the People There, and There; Think how much Better Off You Are than They Are—Your Prosperity and Liberty are Objects of Their Envy; Your Institutions, Models of Their Imitation.*"—It is not the desire to look to the bright side that is blamed, but when a particular suffering, produced by an assigned cause, has been pointed out, the object of many apologists is to turn the eyes of inquirers and judges into any other quarter in preference. If a man's tenants were to come with a general encomium on the prosperity of the country instead of a specified sum, would it be accepted? In a court of justice in an action for damages did ever any such device occur as that of pleading assets in the hands of a third person? There is in fact no country so poor and so wretched in every element of prosperity, in which matter for this argument might not be found. Were the prosperity of the country tenfold as great as at present, the absurdity of the argument would not in the least degree be lessened. Why should the smallest evil be endured which can be cured because others suffer patiently under greater evils? Should the smallest improvement attainable be neglected because others remain contented in a state of still greater inferiority?

"Seriously and pointedly in the character of a bar to any measure of relief, no, nor to the most trivial improvement, can it ever be employed. Suppose a bill brought in for converting an impassable road anywhere into a passable one, would any man stand up to oppose it who could find nothing better to urge against it than the multitude and goodness of the roads we have already? No: when in the character of a serious bar to the measure in hand, be that measure what it may, an argument so palpably inapplicable is employed, it can only be for the purpose of creating a diversion;—of turning aside the minds of men from the subject really in hand to a picture which, by its beauty, it is hoped, may engross the attention of the assembly, and make them forget for the moment for what purpose they came there."[15]

THE QUIETEST, OR NO COMPLAINT.—"A new law of measure being proposed in the character of a remedy for some incontestable abuse or evil, an objection is frequently started to the following effect:—'The measure is unnecessary. Nobody complains of disorder in that shape, in which it is the aim of your measure to propose a remedy to it. But even when *no* cause of complaint has been found to exist, especially under governments which admit of complaints, men have in general not been slow to complain; much less where any just cause of complaint has existed.' The argument amounts to this:—Nobody complains, therefore nobody suffers. It amounts to a veto on all measures of precaution or prevention, and goes to establish a maxim in legislation directly opposed to the most ordinary prudence of common life; it enjoins us to build no parapets to a bridge till the number of accidents has raised a universal clamor."[16]

PROCRASTINATOR'S ARGUMENT—"*Wait a Little; This is Not the Time.*"—This is the common argument of men who, being in reality hostile to a measure, are ashamed or afraid of appearing to be so. *To-day* is the plea—*eternal exclusion* commonly the object. It is the same sort of quirk as a plea of abatement in law—which is never employed but on the side of a dishonest defendant, whose hope it is to obtain an ultimate triumph, by overwhelming his adversary with despair, impoverishment, and lassitude. Which is the properest day to do good? which is the properest day to remove a nuisance? We answer, the very first day a man can be found to propose the removal of it; and whoever opposes the removal of it on that day will (if he dare) oppose it on every other. There is in the minds of many feeble friends to virtue and improvement, an imaginary period for the removal of evils, which it would certainly be worth while to wait for, if there was the smallest chance of its ever arriving—a period of unexampled peace and prosperity, when a patriotic king and an enlightened mob united their ardent efforts for the amelioration of human affairs; when the oppressor is as delighted to give up the oppression, as the oppressed is to be liberated from it; when the difficulty and the unpopularity would be to continue the evil, not to abolish it! These are the periods when fair-weather philosophers are willing to venture out and hazard a little for the general good. But the history of human nature is so contrary to all this, that almost all improvements are made after the bitterest resistance, and in the midst of tumults and civil violence—the worst period at which they can be made, compared to which any period is eligible, and should be seized hold of by the friends of salutary reform.

SNAIL'S PACE ARGUMENT—"*One Thing at a Time!—Not Too Fast!—Slow and Sure!*—Importance of the business—extreme difficulty of the business—danger of innovation—need of caution and circumspection—impossibility of foreseeing all consequences—danger of precipitation—everything should be gradual—one thing at a time—this is not the time—great occupation at present—

wait for more leisure—people well satisfied—no petitions presented—no complaints heard—no such mischief has yet taken place—stay till it has taken place! Such is the prattle which the magpie in office, who, understanding nothing, yet understands that he must have something to say on every subject, shouts out among his auditors as a succedaneum to thought."[17]

VAGUE GENERALITIES.—Vague generalities comprehend a numerous class of fallacies resorted to by those who, in preference to the determinate expressions which they might use, adopt others more vague and indeterminate.

Take, for instance, the terms government, laws, morals, religion. Everybody will admit that there are in the world bad governments, bad laws, bad morals, and bad religions. The bare circumstance, therefore, of being engaged in exposing the defects of government, law, morals, and religion does not of itself afford the slightest presumption that a writer is engaged in anything blamable. If his attack be only directed against that which is bad in each, his efforts may be productive of good to any extent. This essential distinction, however, the defender of abuses uniformly takes care to keep out of sight; and boldly imputes to his antagonists an intention to subvert all *government, law, morals, and religion.* Propose anything with a view to the improvement of the existing practice, in relation to law, government, and religion, he will treat you with an oration upon the necessity and utility of law, government, and religion. Among the several cloudy appellatives which have been commonly employed as cloaks for misgovernment, there is none more conspicuous in this atmosphere of illusion than the word order. As often as any measure is brought forward which has for its object to lessen the sacrifice made by the many to the few, *social order* is the phrase commonly opposed to its progress.

"By a defalcation made from any part of the mass of fictitious delay, vexation, and expense, out of which, and in proportion to which, lawyers' profit is made to flow-by any defalcation made from the mass of needless and worse than useless emolument to office, with or without service or pretence of service—by any addition endeavored to be made to the quantity, or improvement in the quality of service rendered, or time bestowed in service rendered in return for such emolument—by every endeavor that has for its object the persuading the people to place their fate at the disposal of any other agents than those in whose hands breach of trust is certain, due fulfilment of it morally and physically impossible—*social order* is said to be endangered, and threatened to be destroyed."[18]

In the same way "Establishment" is a word in use to protect the bad parts of establishments, by charging those who wish to remove or alter them, with a wish to subvert all good establishments.

Mischievous fallacies also circulate from the convertible use of what Mr. B. is pleased to call dyslogistic and eulogistic terms. Thus, a vast concern is expressed for the "liberty of the press," and the utmost abhorrence of its "licentiousness": but then, by the licentiousness of the press is meant every disclosure by which any abuse is brought to light and exposed to shame—by the "liberty of the press" is meant only publications from which no such inconvenience is to be apprehended; and the fallacy consists in employing the sham approbation of liberty as a mask for the real opposition to all free discussion. To write a pamphlet so ill that nobody will read it; to animadvert in terms so weak and insipid upon great evils, that no disgust is excited at the vice, and no apprehension in the evil-doer, is a fair use of the liberty of the press, and is not only pardoned by the friends of government, but draws from them the most fervent eulogium. The licentiousness of the press consists in doing the thing boldly and well, in striking terror into the guilty, and in rousing the attention of the public to the defence of their highest interests. This is the licentiousness of the press held in the greatest horror by timid and corrupt men, and punished by semi-animous, semi-cadaverous judges, with a captivity of many years. In the same manner the dyslogistic and eulogistic fallacies are used in the case of reform.

"Between all abuses whatsoever there exists that connection—between all persons who see, each of them, any one abuse in which an advantage results to himself, there exists, in point of interest, that close and sufficiently understood connection, of which intimation has been given already. To no one abuse can correction be administered without endangering the existence of every other.

"If, then, with this inward determination not to suffer, so far as depends upon himself, the adoption of any reform which he is able to prevent, it should seem to him necessary or advisable to put on for a cover the profession or appearance of a desire to contribute to such reform—in pursuance of the device or fallacy here in question, he will represent that which goes by the name of reform as distinguishable into two species; one of them a fit subject for approbation, the other for disapprobation. That which he thus professes to have marked for approbation, he will accordingly for the expression of such approbation, characterize by some adjunct of the *eulogistic* cast, such as moderate, for example, or temperate, or practical, or practicable.

"To the other of these nominally distinct species, he will, at the same time, attach some adjunct of the dyslogistic cast, such as violent, intemperate, extravagant, outrageous, theoretical, speculative, and so forth.

"Thus, then, in profession and to appearance, there are in his conception of the matter two distinct and opposite species of reform, to one of which his approbation, to the other his disapprobation, is attached. But the species to which his approbation is attached is an *empty* species—a species in which no individual is, or is intended to be, contained.

"The species to which his disapprobation is attached is, on the contrary, a crowded species, a receptacle in which the whole contents of the *genus*—of the *genus* 'Reform'—are intended to be included."[19]

ANTI-RATIONAL FALLACIES.—When reason is in opposition to a man's interests his study will naturally be to render the faculty itself, and whatever issues from it, an object of hatred and contempt. The sarcasm and other figures of speech employed on the occasion are directed not merely against reason but against thought, as if there were something in the faculty of thought that rendered the exercise of it incompatible with useful and successful practice. Sometimes a plan, which would not suit the official person's interest, is without more ado pronounced a speculative one; and, by this observation, all need of rational and deliberate discussion is considered to be superseded. The first effort of the corruptionist is to fix the epithet speculative upon any scheme which he thinks may cherish the spirit of reform. The expression is hailed with the greatest delight by bad and feeble men, and repeated with the most unwearied energy; and to the word "speculative," by way of reinforcement, are added: *theoretical, visionary, chimerical, romantic, Utopian.*

"Sometimes a distinction is taken, and thereupon a concession made. The plan is good in theory, but it would be bad in practice, *i. e.*, its being good in theory does not hinder its being bad in practice.

"Sometimes, as if in consequence of a further progress made in the art of irrationality, the plan is pronounced to be "too good to be practicable"; and its being so good as it is, is thus represented as the very cause of its being bad in practice.

"In short, such is the perfection at which this art is at length arrived, that the very circumstances of a plan's being susceptible of the appellation of a *plan*, has been gravely stated as a circumstance sufficient to warrant its being rejected—rejected, if not with hatred, at any rate with a sort of accompaniment which, to the million, is commonly felt still more galling—with contempt."[20]

There is a propensity to push theory too far; but what is the just inference? not that theoretical propositions (i.e., all propositions of any considerable comprehension or extent) should, from such their extent, be considered to be false *in toto*, but only that, in the particular case, should inquiry be made whether, supposing the proposition to be in the character of a rule generally true, an exception ought to be taken out of it. It might almost be imagined that there was something wicked or unwise in the exercise of thought; for everybody feels a necessity for disclaiming it. "I am not given to speculation, I am no friend to theories." Can a man disclaim theory, can he disclaim speculation, without disclaiming thought?

The description of persons by whom this fallacy is chiefly employed are those who, regarding a plan as adverse to their interests, and not finding it on the ground of general utility exposed to any preponderant objection, have recourse to this objection in the character of an instrument of contempt, in the view of preventing those from looking into it who might have been otherwise disposed. It is by the fear of seeing it practised that they are drawn to speak of it as impracticable. "Upon the face of it (exclaims some feeble or pensioned gentleman) it carries that air of plausibility, that, if you were not upon your guard, might engage you to bestow more or less attention upon it; but were you to take the trouble, you would find that (as it is with all these plans which promise so much) practicability would at last be wanting to it. To save yourself from this trouble, the wisest course you can take is to put the plan aside, and to think no more about the matter." This is always accompanied with a peculiar grin of triumph.

The whole of these fallacies may be gathered together in a little oration, which we will denominate the "Noodle's Oration":—

"What would our ancestors say to this, Sir? How does this measure tally with their institutions? How does it agree with their experience? Are we to put the wisdom of yesterday in competition with the wisdom of centuries? [*Hear! hear!*] Is beardless youth to show no respect for the decisions of mature age? [*Loud cries of hear! hear!*] If this measure be right, would it have escaped the wisdom of those Saxon progenitors to whom we are indebted for so many of our best political institutions? Would the Dane have passed it over? Would the Norman have rejected it? Would such a notable discovery have been reserved for these modern and degenerate times? Besides, Sir, if the measure itself is good, I ask the honorable gentleman if this is the time for carrying it into execution—whether, in fact, a more unfortunate period could have been selected than that which he has chosen? If this were an ordinary measure I should not oppose it with so much vehemence; but, Sir, it calls in question the wisdom of an irrevocable law—of a law passed at the memorable period of the Revolution. What right have we, Sir, to break down this firm column on which the great men of that age stamped a character of eternity? Are not all authorities against this measure—Pitt, Fox, Cicero, and the Attorney—and Solicitor—General? The proposition is new, Sir; it is the first time it was ever heard in this House. I am not prepared, Sir—this House is not prepared—to receive it. The measure implies a distrust of his Majesty's Government; their disapproval is sufficient to warrant opposition. Precaution only is requisite where danger is apprehended. Here the high character of the individuals in question is a sufficient guarantee against any ground of alarm. Give not, then, your sanction to this measure; for, whatever be its character, if you do give your sanction to it, the same man by whom this is proposed will propose to you others to which it will be impossible to give your consent. I care very little, Sir, for the ostensible measure; but what is there behind? What are the honorable gentleman's future schemes? If we pass this bill, what fresh concessions may he not require? What further degradation is he planning for his country? Talk of evil and inconvenience, Sir! look to other countries—study other aggregations and societies of men, and then see whether the laws of this country demand a remedy or deserve a panegyric. Was the honorable gentleman (let me ask him) always of this way of thinking? Do I not remember when he was the advocate, in this House, of very opposite opinions? I not only quarrel with his present sentiments, Sir, but I declare very frankly I do not like the party with which he acts. If his own motives were as pure as possible, they cannot but suffer contamination from those with whom he is politically associated. This measure may be a boon to the Constitution, but I will accept no favor to the Constitution from such hands. [*Loud cries of hear! hear!*] I profess myself, Sir, an honest and upright member of the British Parliament, and I am not afraid to profess myself an enemy to all change and all innovation. I am satisfied with things as they are; and it will be my pride and pleasure to hand down this country to my children as I received it from those who preceded me. The honorable gentleman pretends to justify the severity with which he has attacked the noble lord who presides in the Court of Chancery. But I say such attacks are pregnant with mischief to government itself. Oppose ministers, you oppose government; disgrace ministers, you disgrace government; bring ministers into contempt, you bring government into contempt; and anarchy and civil war are the consequences. Besides, sir, the measure is unnecessary. Nobody complains of disorder in that shape in which it is the aim of your measure to propose a remedy to it. The business is one of the greatest importance; there is need of the greatest caution and circumspection. Do not let us be precipitate, Sir; it is impossible to foresee all consequences. Everything should be gradual; the example of a neighboring nation should fill us with alarm! The honorable gentleman has taxed me with illiberality, Sir; I deny the charge. I hate innovation, but I love improvement. I am an enemy to the corruption of government, but I defend its influence. I dread reform, but I dread it only when it is intemperate. I consider the liberty of the press as the great palladium of the Constitution; but, at the same time, I hold the licentiousness of the press in the greatest abhorrence. Nobody is more conscious than I am of the splendid abilities of the honorable mover, but I tell him at once his scheme is too good to be practicable. It savors of Utopia. It looks well in theory, but it won't do in practice. It will not do, I repeat, Sir, in practice; and so the advocates of the measure will find, if, unfortunately, it should find its way through Parliament. [*Cheers.*] The source of that corruption to which the honorable member alludes is in the minds of the people; so rank and extensive is that corruption, that no political reform can have any effect in removing it. Instead of reforming others—instead of reforming the State, the Constitution, and everything that is most excellent, let each man reform himself! let him look at home, he will find there enough to do without looking abroad and aiming at what is out of his power. [Loud cheers.] And now, Sir, as it is frequently the custom in this House to end with a quotation, and as the gentleman who preceded me in the debate has anticipated me in my favorite quotation of the 'Strong pull and the long pull,' I shall end with the memorable words of the assembled barons: '*Nolumus leges Angliæ mutari.*[21]

"Upon the whole, the following are the characters which appertain in common to all the several arguments here distinguished by the name of fallacies:—

"1. Whatsoever be the measure in hand, they are, with relation to it, irrelevant.

"2. They are all of them such, that the application of these irrelevant arguments affords a presumption either of the weakness or total absence of relevant arguments on the side of which they are employed.

"3. To any good purpose they are all of them unnecessary.

"4. They are all of them not only capable of being applied, but actually in the habit of being applied, and with advantage, to bad purposes, viz.: to the obstruction and defeat of all such measures as have for their object the removal of the abuses or other imperfections still discernible in the frame and practice of the government.

"5. By means of the irrelevancy, they all of them consume and misapply time, thereby obstructing the course and retarding the progress of all necessary and useful business.

"6. By that irritative quality which, in virtue of their irrelevancy, with the improbity or weakness of which it is indicative, they possess, all of them, in a degree more or less considerable, but in a more particular degree such of them as consist in personalities, are productive of ill-humor, which in some instances has been productive of bloodshed, and is continually productive, as above, of waste of time and hindrance of business.

"7. On the part of those who, whether in spoken or written discourses, give utterance to them, they are destined to operate.

"8. On the part of those on whom they operate, they are indicative either of improbity or intellectual weakness, or of a contempt for the understanding of those on whose minds they are indicative of intellectual weakness; and on the part of those in and by whom they are pretended to operate, they are indicative of improbity, viz., in the shape of insincerity.

"The practical conclusion is, that in proportion as the acceptance, and thence the utterance, of them can be prevented, the understanding of the public will be strengthened, the morals of the public will be purified, and the practice of government improved."[22]

[1] A review of "The Book of Fallacies: from Unfinished Papers of Jeremy Bentham. By a Friend. London, 1824."

[2] "Other things being equal."

[3] "Not to-day!"

[4] From Bentham, pp. 74–77.

[5] *Ibid.*, pp. 84–86.

[6] *Ibid.*, pp. 110, 111.

[7] *Ibid.*, p. 120.

[8] "If that were so, I should be only a happy accident."

[9] *Ibid.*, pp. 123, 124.

[10] *Ibid.*, pp. 125, 126.

[11] *Ibid.*, pp. 132, 133.

[12] *Ibid.*, pp. 141, 142.

[13] *Ibid.*, pp. 162, 163.

[14] *Ibid.*, pp. 185, 186.

[15] *Ibid.*, pp. 196, 197.

[16] *Ibid.*, pp. 190, 191.

[17] *Ibid.*, pp. 203, 204.

[18] *Ibid.*, p. 234.

[19] *Ibid.*, pp. 277, 278.

[20] *Ibid.*, p. 296.

[21] "We do not wish the laws of England to be changed."

[22] From Bentham, pp. 359, 360.